T0077460

The publication of this book has in part been made possible by a donation from The Coach House Fund.

THE
MUSHROOM SUMMER
of SKIPPER DARLING

POEMS BY

TONY VOSS

CRANE RIVER

London • Cape Town

2019

ACKNOWLEDGEMENTS

Acknowledgement is due to the following journals in which some of these poems first appeared: *Carapace, New African, New Contrast, New Coin, Rhodesian Poetry, Rhodian* and *Stanzas*, and to the AVBOB Poetry Project website.

I have many people to thank for the attention and love that have given me readers. I thank especially my wife, Carol, and our children, Lucy, Ben, Jonathan, Andrew and Aurora. Many poets have served as examples and offered encouragement. For the sympathy of a contemporary fellow poet and the rigour of a wise reader, I thank Douglas Reid Skinner.

Published in Cape Town, South Africa by Crane River in 2019

ISBN: 978-0-620-83127-7

Layout by Crane River Design
Produced and distributed by uHlanga

Cover design by Nick Mulgrew

CONTENTS

I

II

III

IV

V (SONNETS)

I

Bats

Standing on the loud landing
of the fire escape, we reached
with tennis racquets for the bats.
They came like Heinkels over the oaks,

making their own way to the soft
fruit in the orchard, or the grapes,
the hanepoot, loading the vine.
Perhaps they roosted in the loft

of the chapel in the courtyard.
I never saw a bat brought down.
The sweet Cape night was the world
before words, the code unbroken.

First Snow

Snow was that word until my year of ten.
A day and a night's journey from the sea
and boarding school, the train stopped at
De Aar, where we waited for the connection
to German South-West, along a line laid
in wartime at a mile a day. By then

we were in civvies, and the carriages
a caravan of privilege. I would wake
in a warm middle bunk to the smell
of coffee: in the dining car, the menu
promised, "Passengers are entitled
to a liberal helping of all the dishes."

At that cemetery of steam and signal
box of histories, Olive Schreiner sojourned
cool seasons of the peace: restlessly
we watched Alan Ladd in *The Great Gatsby*
at the Criterion. You could buy the *Strand
Magazine* at the station bookstall.

One July night, after cold handshakes
to those travelling to other quarters,
and shivering among uniforms of black
and brown, the hiss and crash and shriek
of shunting, and following porters
to our last train, my first snow fell, in flakes

of light and silence over the sombre
yards and the camps beyond. I took it
for a miracle, neither foam nor cotton
wool, and I knew we were at home and on
our way home – even if snow never came down
again. Then we pulled out into the winter

night and that snow stretched – our dust of snow –
out around us, melting against the windows,
and as the small lights of dim Karoo stations
passed from the darkness into memory,
the train of snow whispered: "You thought we were
dreaming, and we are watching over you."

Things

Come out of the thunderous afternoon
into the cupboard under the stairs;
avoid the clubs and spears, silent
sentinels at the door, and move among
these trunks and lamps and photographs
into the still life of things, where I
am searching for our past. Things
grow out of this darkness: in the cool
deep reaches we may find statues,
lilies, icons, and the encroaching earth.

(Your guests are running up the stairs
above our heads: the noise of their coming –
men and women of particular skills,
graces, and nervous habits – thunders
through the hollow roof-tree of your house.)
Here is a child's drum; here is a chest
of Knysna wood inlaid with ivory;
it is full of old papers: these mean
and yellowing magazines are loaded
with old poems. (The voices of old friends.)

It is the one voice of others calls us
from our nacreous bed, weeping, naked
as a statue and a lily. The words are old.
The thunder lingers in the still life of things.

In the Studio

Outside, the winter dark, the sky-
sounding sea, all-night trains threading
the coast, crane flower pecking
at stained glass. Inside, you and I,

friends who once shared a name,
talk of old love and separate lives,
by the light of oils and water-
colours. On the easel, shallow foam

recedes across a silver beach
towards tomorrow's morning
horizon. As our history
takes its shape and toll, rash

memories of kissing overtake
the salt taste of betrayal. Now,
while our first child awaits the birth
of her first child, we speak

to celebrate the wordless
elements of peace, in lines
acknowledging the scrupulous
intimacy of sea and sky.

Palimpsest

Focus on the shallow pane
as if it were the air:
see the steady eye, the wing tips
raised in panic. In prayer?

A ring dove taken by surprise,
into its own reflection.
Dusting an imprint on the glass –
a state of resurrection –

the creature could not pierce the prism.
Where did it hover next?
Does it survive the cataclysm
only in this text?

Or rise up from the strawberry bed
into the fig tree? And fly
over the veld to the lands, and the dam's
kind mirror of the sky.

Rod

This winter morning dew shines on a line
of cold green piping lying prone, sheathing
a longer (by, say, half a metre) fine
copper cable cauterised onto a bar
of grey steel sunk into red soil. A pair

of uprights springs from concrete still setting
in the earth. Now the footing is secure,
two men lift the sleek cylinder to swing
on a bolt running through the hollow pole
and one of two pairs of opposed holes

in the staff itself. A bright hawser (from
a winch in the truck) is hooked to a hasp
fused to the post, a metre up. Four arms
ready the baton between the stanchions.
As the team struggles to steady the shaft,

André manages the truck and controls
the winch, Thabelo rallies and works
with the men. The crew pushes, the winch pulls
(raising the standard) until the whole feline
filament's in tune. As Johnny aligns

the second bolt and spanners in the two,
Lesitja welds in place the singing switch.
In good time for Limpopo's summer storms,
the lightning rod is reaching for the blue,
standing up for the dark hazardous thatch.

Lightning Scene

Beloved! The lightning flickers, its fingers flashing
     for friendship and love in the dark heart of the city,
Blazing like the huddled hearth of a cold night watchman
     who fills his rusty oil drum with summer's dry leavings.
We lay there, you and I, as the earth shook in Seaview:
     we watched the distance glooming, expecting the thunder,
Bringing rain to the Point and the Bay from Umgeni,
     hiding the harbour, to Brighton Beach on the littoral.
Over the steep Berea the airborne ocean rushed
     and poor houses sank to earth in Cato Manor beyond,
As the drift of waters passed into Kloof and KwaMashu,
     scattering wisdom monkeys from their restless refuge.
In gardens, gazebos, in parks, palms and pavilions
     fell to the scythe of the storm, birds flew from their cages.
Temples of Shiva shifted, foreseeing Nirvana,
     temples of mammon shivered, on rocky foundations.
The clouds shed their burden on Umlazi and Chatsworth,
     like Bhagwan the tailor unfolding the bales of his fabric.
Towers of light the next day from the Bluff to Umhlanga
     were spun with the flood-borne wrack like the floss of candy.
At daybreak we woke to mousebird and barbet calling
     as if they had drunk all night in the moonlit cane.
At dusk drowned mongooses lay where the torrent had left them,
     high up the valley wall, dead, on the squills and lilies.

Flashes

1   PASSION FRUIT

Woken by thunder, tempted by lightning,
the child stands at the low window, to guard
the yard reaching to the boundary wall

below the looming corrugated iron
roof of the Apostoliese Geloof-
sending Kerk, before the next roll shining

like a sea in the sheen of rain, the sheaves
of light, the granadilla flashing
stark blossoms on the emerald leaves –

hearing the mother's story of the passion:
The veil of the temple was rent in twain.

2   ON THE FENCE

Heading west from Halcyon Drift, south under
the Witteberg, north to Lady Grey, on
our way to Herschel where Olive Schreiner

first saw the light, horizontal flashes
and the roar of a city at its limits,
bringing advance news of weather, bushes

shivering, the air suddenly cold, thunder
rolling the Morris into shelter just short
of a barbed-wire fence, which grabbed the lightning

from us in a prophetic neon scrawl:
like glowing metal in the midst of fire.

3   ONLY THE LIGHTNING

She jerks the Johnson two-stroke into gear,
a singing lesson ringing in her head,
clouds closing the sky as she leaves the mooring,

and the storm breaking its waters into
the dusk, parents wondering by the window
through the struggling glow, staring into dark

thunder and fractal flashes reflected,
frightening, dividing sea from sky, bobbing
across the stricken sound, only the lightning

bringing the hope of daylight to the night:
a way for the lightning of the thunder.

4   NEW YEAR'S EVE

South, from the harbour bridge, midnight rumour
of harsh cordite and high celebration,
making a horizon of the headland,

fireworks, mirrored, east from the verandah,
by heavy cloud, raised from the Pacific's
dark sea line by parallels of lightning,

unheard bars of thunder, the starlit sky
between covering our quiet vigil,
by a safe harbour, distant from family

and friends, the last wine silvering the flutes:
lightning, and thunder, and voices.

The Mushroom Summer of Skipper Darling

– Grahamstown, 1955

There is a time to remember the wise
and mythical skills
of Skipper Darling, night watchman
of the Eastern Hills.

He could divine mushrooms in the hollow
dark. Armed only with a torch,
on deep summer nights he would lead us out
across the bottle-green fields of Albany –
pitches and meadows – lying like velvet
to the touch. Rooted in his black figure,
shielding it, the wand of light leapt from face
to face. From grove to echoing grove
of mushrooms, that took their shape, seemed
to take their being from that bright spear.
Halfmense. Lilliputians, giving only
a damp cough as we plucked them, silent
to his histrionic gestures. When the last
switch telescoped the light we knew the basket
full. Whispering, we returned,
to feast on mushrooms and bilious *Jubilee*:
new pagans in the misshapen light
of our midnight room.

Moonless night. The scorpion memory
is dying on its sting.
Was it not wisdom but the torch
that made him king?

II

In My Country

in my country, the sea is green
and roadside grass is red

there is no word for queue
and many calls for bird

in my country, the heroes have no names
but they are not forgotten

the people hear their voices
in the sweet air we breathe

in my country, the sky is haunted
by the memory of rain

and with the evening, children
dance to the music of the fish

in my country, we eat together
and work in the harmony of hope

knowing the doors will always open
to the seed among the stones

in my country, stars are constant,
shining on the castles and the fields

horsemen celebrate the city
to follow the customs of the dawn

in my country, if I share
my dream with a stranger

or a traveller she becomes
the one who will fulfil my dream

Map Reading

In a way you will know where you are:
the road is marked by ruins, the verdure
of presences, which you will recognise

as you pass. It is not a long journey
but some have never made it. Every year
magnetic north declines and you will need

to make appropriate calculations.
There may be a difference of almost
a generation between the sheets. Certain

points looked fixed, but even the Olievenberg
is featureless without windmills, footpaths,
hedges. The salient colours of the map

suggest that in this latitude you will
rely on the sun for a true reading.
The long way round may be the journey home.

Nieu Bethesda

Climbing the pass into the early winter
we found a fountain frozen to a fence,
the wasting water saved by a cold hand.

These dusty latitudes of trust overlap
the unlettered regions of surmise. Do not
abandon the alphabet of self-assurance,

or the harmonies of composure, but
with your eyes on the Compassberg, reckon
the horizon of hospitality.

This last settlement surrounds a steeple:
green documents chequered on a spike.
Time your arrival for the crepuscule

of dawn or afternoon: the chased monuments
of enlightenment will not be read
in the vertical glare of midday.

Waiting for the Train

Each day at the station
widows and porters stand,
like the train itself
waiting for the train.
The timetable peels
from Africa's body
like a dirty sheet
that cannot protect her
from our leisurely sights
trained on the monuments
and the installations.

At the mines the smell
of fire haunts the air,
like the train itself.
Praying for rain
we watched the ministers
and chiefs pass by –
we thought of skirted soldiers
dancing on their swords.
After the paper smiles
they whisper golden words
hearing the moles below.

"The ostriches give way
to lions very soon:
figs burst on the air,
birds scatter the sun."
Like the rain itself,
praying for the rain,
her musing body heaves,
timeless to know or see
what fire hangs between
the painted tourist and
the terrorist in me.

Sunday Morning

The bells, the letting go. The Bel-
mont Valley road shakes our station
wagon out of Grahamstown, not
making wagons now. The Blaauwkrantz Bridge –

here, in nineteen-eleven,
Hazel Smith, clutching at steel,
clung with her other hand to her still-
younger brother. In the pool

below, *Abantu Bamlambo*
were there to welcome the stock-fair
passengers in the last coach
as it fell. After disaster,

the letting go, the bells. Beyond
the cutting, past the cricket field,
people are selling prickly pears.
"Peel them first, the spines are sharp.

Take this knife." Behind the hedge,
the farmers are appealing. "See,
children, here we can hear the sea.
Beware the backwash. Bathe between

the flags." Through the beach bush the young
men come, shouldering high fighting sticks.
Who has not heard their steps and songs,
the bells, the letting go?

Cricket Country

SHAW PARK, 8.30am
Red-billed ground hoopoe in the *Erythrina*
calls for the openers to take the green;
dew sheens the grass, the moon lingers
as the sun climbs over the sight screen.
The sea breeze rising will swerve the swingers.

MANLEY FLATS, 10.30am
The farmers' wives are serving tea and cakes
to relatives and artisans and clerks.
At deep fine leg (or is it deep mid off?),
I hear the sea beyond the loerie's cough.
The skipper calls the spinner for his breaks.

SALEM, 4pm
Westering rays behind the scorers shine
on chapel window and keen graveyard stone.
Here, where a family can field a team,
a batsman keeps his lineage and his line
now gentlemen and shepherds play the game.

SOUTHWELL, 5.30pm
St. James's Church drops a reluctant shadow
on the mown ellipse, cut from rough meadow.
This boundary on the frontier of the day
marks all the promise of tomorrow:
in dreams we hear the umpire calling, "Play!"

At Nongqawuse's Grave

Scanning the tilted field, a harvester
levels lucerne. Native trees and bush
bunch at the centre like a posy,
tall heads that are not cropped. In this grove

"…lies Nongqause …" – girl-woman
of the waters' voice.
Over the dunes the sea
beats at Boknes and Diaz Point:

neighbours' cattle pant and prosper.
After the Island, she lived
here, among labourers. And died
forty years beyond apocalypse.

Two Birds with Stone

– after Roberts

1

The thrush of Kurrichane is somewhat shy,
rehearsing an eccentric song in spring,
straying from riparian bush to dry
forest, from the sure trees descending

only to search for food; runs, stops, tics
a wing, listens, plunges an orange beak
into the earth. The nest high in a fork
is a basin fashioned of grass, roots, twigs,

dried leaves and string, fine-lined with thistle,
mudstuck to a right branch. Before masons
came, thrush settled here, with the sweet whistle,
and stayed, among the long-abandoned stones.

2

In Latakoo the singing bush lark falls,
and rises on the air, a madrigal
of praise, at whim imitating the calls
of working neighbours and rare travellers;

le-Khuku, kiewietjie, bee-eater, chat,
Jangroentjie, tsemeli. Scraping a nest
in the veld, hidden between shy tufts, tat-
and grass-lined, the lark finds slender rest.

All the airs tell us, this is our skylark:
perching on green steps of old stone cities,
lark has something to say, recalls the ark,
chases the skies, waiting for sunrise.

Acropolis

The place of stone
is between earth and sky,
was far from water,
close to the sun's eye.

The dry stone wall will
fall, when it will fall,
to dust and fill.
Now it rises, all

surprising as a tree:
the frieze and tower,
the turrets and free-
standing stones hover

like drums and fingers
in the morning. (What
masons and singers
made these lines?) Not

a ruin, but the unknown
city in construction.
The place of stone
is between stone and stone.

Sandstone

Sometimes the capitol will find dimension
stone in a far province, south, across the river.
Masons can smell it there, and after rain,

the sandstone shines, but in our station,
in our church, the school, the old hotel,
stone addresses the air. We're on a railhead,

close enough to be economical:
seeing the stone, the architect could tell.
Shaping the stone, the masons push dry slips

into a chiselled trough or into holes
drilled in sweet patterns on the level face
of the earthbound stone. They pour the river

water over the shims, and the swelling wood
cracks the soft sandstone along honest lines
made by their easy sequence of drilled holes.

Let us respect the earth, find green acres
for the plough, food and shelter for the poor.
Let us also raise strong teams of masons,

to beautify in stone our avenues.
When you travel to the city you will see
the light of home in the dimension stone.

Orpheus at Nylstroom

The doves were calling "*vukutu*" – the oaks
were green, when she was taken from that grand
and sensual house among the vines. The books
were barren, the folk came silent from the land.
I left on this journey in the first weeks
of summer. To the east, the ocean roared
above its spoils. (White ladies still appear
to sailors there and ghosts of sailors guard
that margin of the Indian career.)
Memory of her only drives me onward.
My body withers to a weathered sign.

There were rivers in the distance somewhere,
the urgent traffic on its beat
of seasons, when I met a surveyor.
He came like a mirror from the heat.
His eyes rattled. Shaken with ban and prayer,
he rumoured of gold and diamonds – nations
herded to famine by revenge and prophecy.
For three days we shared our rations,
until he made one with a lion-hunting party.
Shouldering spears, loaded into a truck,
they drove off into the dust like a hedgehog.

An old man's story of Ukcombekantsini
snores in my memory like hearsay:
"All the chief's wives bore sons but one, and she
was barren and alone; until one day
the doves brought her twins in a basket.
The boy was white. The girl was very shining."
Wine and cemeteries are far from these farmers
who flatter the air: tall warriors; lissom
women. Surely it is the same country:
now I approach the echoing prison
where she lies, dreaming of a field-encircled city.

Long Walk

In the gathering cold of autumn, no hint of rain,
travelling north towards the Lootsberg pass,
I had the wheel of the family saloon.

He was walking south, filling his one-car lane
as if all traffic were still moving at the pace
of *trekboer*, ox and *disselboom*.

If he had turned to notice us, as I allowed
my eyes to leave the road without loss of speed,
his breath would have misted the Shatterprufe.

But he took no time; we were too loud,
too reckless, and he had a deeper need:
to a destination like a seismograph

he had been walking for two hundred years.
I recognised his uniform from memory:
he wore a short blue combat jacket,

a light waistcoat and loose grey trousers;
his hat was a gesture to the Regency,
over a headscarf, like a pirate;

barefoot, a red bandanna at his throat.
Somewhere up there, where he vanishes
into the rear-view mirror, he is a beau:

his ears are dressed with rings, a sharp stole
fanfares around his neck, a bouquet
of ostrich feathers flutters to and fro.

He dances lightly along, rejoicing
in panache, looking eagerly ahead,
lifted above the ground. And we are free.

Alexander Urinator

1 FAKIR

I asked the fakir, "Is the world
no more than imagination,
idea?" He brought me to a *ghat*
here on the bank of the river
where we stripped naked and entered
the water to the waist. "Now dive,"
he said, "deep, under the water,
just for a moment." And I dived.

What did I see in that descent?
Forgetting kingly consciousness
I saw myself, a labourer
with many children, all starving,
and a wife, ill and miserable
as I, all the cares of the world
upon us. Each day seemed to bring
yet more terrible disasters.

But I gave a start and emptied
my lungs, and behold! I am back
on the bank, emperor once more,
dripping along with the fakir.
This is a wonder surpassing
the Hindu Kush, Persepolis
and all the beautiful cities
I have named Eskanderia.

2 GYMNOSOPHIST

"How long do you think it decent
for a man to live?"
                          Till death appear
more desirable than life.
"Then he that conquers an empire
will order an exact survey
of the lands."
                    Does he think to take
exact survey of his conscience?
We call what he has a man's means,
but that is truly his means, how
he came by what he has. How few
(when a state comes to any great
proportion) know that? Who know
what they have, what they are worth?

"One philosopher thinks he has dived
to the bottom, when he says he knows
nothing. And yet another thinks
that he knows more when he replies,
'You do not know so much, you know
nothing.' The prophet thinks himself
wise because he does not know."
                                      If
you know that every riotous
Macedonian feast cuts off a year
and every wanton Persian night
seven years of your seventy,
that would take you some degree
towards perfection in knowledge.

3 POET

He reached the tree of everlasting life.

He rose to heaven in a magic chariot
pulled by griffins.

He sinks below the sea in a crystal bell
and the fish crowd around to pay homage.

The Memory of Horse

In '91, Jacob van Reenen crossed
the Xora, at a distance from the sea
of about two hours. Caught sight of a horse

belonging to the farmer Doris
Potgieter, lost during a journey
undertaken seven years before

to those same castaways he had returned
to find. The creature was wild, running
with a herd of elands, and was pursued

until they caught it. The next morning
the bay had once more become so tame
that it was mounted again.

People still call that place
Tafelehashe,
The Heights of Horse.

Swimming the Horses

Quite early, once the chill is off the air
pennants of mist still waving on the water,
a groom will walk a new horse to the river
to meet the trainer, already waiting there.

Whistles, words, and whinnies making conversation,
on the soft bank the two exchange their charges:
the groom returns a swum horse to the stable,
the trainer leads a dry horse to the water.

Fronting the horse, he backs into the river
leading the patient creature by example:
gently the water takes them up together.
Over the deep their wash is clear and simple.

Sometimes, he swims the horses from a dory,
rowed by an upright oarsman facing forward,
the shafts in high rowlocks. The trainer,
from the stern, seems to tell the horse a story,

whispering and murmuring with the boatman's rhythm.
In Montaigne's essay 'Of the Cannibals',
the man who first brought horses to those people,
although he had been often in their country,

and engaged in civil conversation,
so horrified them that before they could take notice
they slew him there and then with arrows.
Still, in this river, we will swim the horses

bringing them safely to the green horizon,
to bless us with their faith and dignity.
Submitting to ungainly purposes,
they swim in innocence.

On the Beach at Sezela

– for Cherry Clayton

They do not look each other in the eye,
but gaze at her from separate solitudes,
remembering the bonfires on the sand,
the smoking mill, the mirrors of the past.

From left to right. Plomer knits his way home
to Bloomsbury and inscrutability.
Campbell, bearded, balding, stands hat in hand,
a poor white seeking work. Van der Post

is holding up his trousers as he aims
into the bright eye of Africa. Flames
illumine her, spectator at this feast.
Dark voices roll the rivers to the coast.

I miss old Big Mouth most.

Sixties Conversations

      – for Harry Cohen

1 THE JUGGLER

I'd seen you last, before you disappeared,
between two plainclothes cops, in Cora Terrace,
looking on the Bay. We follow choices.
Yours threatened torture and detention; then,
in what passed for plain daylight, banning

and the exit permit. Now, word by word,
far from that frontier, our early talk falls
into place: of listening devices,
telephone campaigns to block security
lines. I never joined. Was I running

from the blast? Here at your northern barrier
we meet again; the *Blade Runner* poster
dominates the wall: tall windows harmonise
streetlamp and hearth. (Did you complete
Technocracy, your prophetic game of chance,

for taking over the world?) Edinburgh
winter coming on, the Scotch rising,
we talk quietly in a well-lit house
of your children's Lothian accent,
of nationalism, science fiction, nuance

of hummus and haloumi, while the dew
of dinner drifts across the hall. Resistance
and commitment are in the air, closing in
on our pastime conversation.
As if reaching for a cigarette,

you turn away: "Hey! Look what I can do!"
When you spin round to face me you're juggling:
three harlequin balls bounce and float between
us, our eyes meeting through the tracery.
"I learned in prison, how do I forget?"

2 A WALK IN WARRISTON CEMETERY

From new, still-tended graves through the forest
of obelisks we walked into green disorder
and petrified neglect. Ruin had fallen
like a season there on silent

missionaries, illegible writers, passé
inventors, mute women, infants. You say,
"Vandals do this work of nature; out-of-work,
working-class kids, high on glue, unpicking

sepulchres, feel nothing for the final
private property of these dead." (*Famous
wherever the gear that bears his name
engages. A pillar of the faith*

in Africa. Beloved.) By the gate we turn
onto a derailed cutting. Alert,
a shadow trots into a tunnel, emerging
fox in twilight focus. Imagine.

Survival is the whole work of fox.
Echoing on the homely Scottish block,
our words of youth in Africa recall
Cape hunting dog and golden jackal.

Obiter Dicta

– for Douglas Livingstone

1 SEA PITCH

In an ideal world there would be no waste,
no pollution either; on this planet,
mainly polluted by humanity,
family planning is waste management.
Consigning dross and excess to the waves
we trust in microbes for our sanity,
and shape our presence to remembered lives:
in paradise there would be no more sea.
Each new predation of the interloper
sends us in search of supra-vital stains,
demanding of us what is right and proper.
Both birth and death are judged by their remains.
On the blue fields that roll beyond the roads
will we remember that we once were gods?

2 NEWS FROM A FAR COUNTRY: THE KING IS DEAD

The port of palms, a string of suburbs tossed
off the back of a reef-bound train, gateway
to India, dolphin and sunshine coast
of nightmares and the ride of Ndongeni.
Now grey steel waders prey about the bay,
the darkling city lights its early sky,
and from Isipingo to Umgeni
the measured rivers of one life are dry.
On shoals of exile I re-read his charts,
rejoicing in their legendary precision.
Seamanship and rhyme are sister arts:
poetry can take you home, like navigation.
He made his pilgrimage of wind and drift:
the Goodman, Clark and Elvis of his craft.

Forgetting how absolute you made your line,
"Howzit?" (with dialectal schwa) I'd call,
half-greeting and half-summons. "It's fine:
the rest of me's the problem." Now I recall
how on the edge you stood up to reckon
the duty of a gentleman, and in
that blazing barn: "I am a white African,
I must believe this or I must get out."
Didn't you say you'd never cross this bar
without somewhere else to go and a jar
of rough red in the boot? A steady graph
from swing and Singapore. Now I'm half
expecting to see you at the movies:
shades, seersucker jacket, charcoal stovies.

4 THE THRACIAN HORSEMAN

Here, at the last citadel and tower,
where the brown river meets the Indian sea,
I rode in service of Zalmoxis,
the hidden god not mocked by effigy.
Aboard my horse, indigo cloak spreading
for a sail, I surfed the plains. Seasonal
rumours of empire dogged me, receding
over kind gruel flavoured with fennel
and hearth-roasted grains. Always far from home,
I find serenity in the light fall
of leaves, the rise and fracture of foam,
the trust of this infernal animal.
Do not fear death, but celebrate the end –
cadence of snow elated by the wind.

The Poets

– for Sydney Clouts

They return to memory,
like stories of cheetah
in suburban gardens.
From the verandah

where we chatter
through the tall summer evening
we hear suave voices
in the kitchen, singing:

"You deserve to be greatly
loved." When two or three
hunker on the bare floor
of an abandoned house,

they charm the hard
winter, throwing
the last pine cones
onto a candid hearth.

Pumping

– i.m. Rob Amato

Now, at the five-year trough, the creek is dry,
old and self-absorbed. I can find no ponds
among the stones. Shake out the hose and check
the joints: a ritual that acknowledges
the quiet fissure's generosity.
The world's armature protrudes, through a light
integument of dry and patient earth.

We cross the bush path to ask Wayne for help.
Our reserve tank's so low we must suspend
his noisy and neighbourly two-stroke pump
from parallel broomsticks across the narrow mouth
to reach the water level. The concrete
boom transmits a trickle to the tin
house tank. The last few litres of our store.

Turn to the breathing tide, that on its rise
brings us the skates and silver jellyfish,
and leaves us for its fall battalions
of soldier crabs in blue. Can we ignore
such gifts? Swallows swing about the moorings,
today's last ferry calls back to the bittern,
a family of ducks survives the summer.

When the rains came we thought our house would float:
our peri-urban offshore neighbourhood
lost all distinction in the clouds' relief.
Wayne's steps were like a Villa d'Este fountain,

the creek pools disappeared again beneath
its flow, frogs spoke up in the shoreline grass.
A neighbour called to share the local lore

with newcomers: "Easy on the water;
after heavy rain, too much domestic
usage strains the bay. Watch the septic tank."
His beard is silvered with the fall: I see
electrolysis on our outboard's
sacrificial anode, crusty seaweed
on a buoy. This world is our dwelling place.

Dear Rob, I send you back your story
across the elements that fall between us,
hoping that in these lines I find its time.
In a sweltering Highveld summer, stuck
to the truant darkness of the Regal
Bio Café, you were watching the last reel
of *The Treasure of Sierra Madre*,

that *Pardoner's Tale* for our youth. A few
more frames of desert to the rail. Fred Dobbs
(alias Humphrey Bogart), dying of thirst,
can hardly speak his new mortality.
From an unseen *laaitie* in the front row
(Any closer and your name's in the programme!)
a dry voice pleaded, "Suck stones, man! Suck stones!"

IV

Skate

(a letter from Australia)

— *to Mike Hickson*

Dear Mike
          I'm a long way from the lagoons
of adolescence, deep in the bars and pitches
of late middle-age, but now and again
a choice encounter brings it all back here.
This morning, wading home after the turn
of the high tide, I checked a splayed shade

cross the sand. He glides away – I'll tune him
no grief, never. Purple with a sheen,
he's been at the Brylcreem. His head is tight
between his kif pecs, waving and clapping,
to fly him through the water. He's sharp,
a pair of flares in motion. A stingray? Hey,

I'll call him skate. Has he lost something
that Smithy judges him degenerate?
Is he in a class with sharks? Skates have
their own family. He's more like a kite
than a guitar, no *sandkruiper*.
A littoralist, bottom-dweller fella

feeding in the crowded shallows, hence
the camouflage. I suppose he's a male,
an *ou*: most skates are. It's hard for aunties
to be completely cartilaginous.

I remember in the band when I played
string bass, back from a smoke break and Art,
signalling us to strike up Waldteufel,
breathed at the mike: "Everybody skate… mate."
Skate's a midlife style, not a language thing.
So, thanks for roaring my forties – naughties,

when I was between families. Bleak years
of emergency, uncouth moments
of hedonism. Thanks for honky-tonk Texans
(I was a *roker* then) and the safe skyfs
of dagga that made me lose my threads. You'd
never have let me marry your sister, mister.

What kept us out of jail? Now I could use
a hot fish curry and a cold Castle
from the Cumberland, keeping my end up
the whole long arvie. Like Neil Harvey.
                                        Gawie.

The Refugees

Drought and long wars drove us from the littoral,
plotting rocky paths to the escarpment.
Having surmised that rain came from the mountains,

we were surprised by the dryness of the highlands.
Creatures in caves were evidence that others
had seen before us and made celebration.

With shallow graves we fertilised the valleys,
leaving behind us vain and idle harvests,
learning what we could not till then have gathered –

it cannot be the soul that makes us human:
only the body and the soul in union.
Beyond that union we are body only.

We were our own and only sustenance:
in our survival metaphor made literal.

The Emigrants

Like the red foxes landed by the gentry,
rabbits and dung beetles, fences and vines,
camels and Macca's, we hail from a long line
of strangers who have made themselves at home,
come to terms with dispersal, bushfire, earthquake,
Vietnam, the Gulf, East Timor, Afghanistan.
Out of this world there is no lucky country.

You soon get used to the pacific weather,
strange trees, long beaches and the sun. Even
in the morning-after banter of parrot,
kookaburra, and cockatoo, always
rehearsing, always getting their act
together, never taking it on the road,
the melody of welcome is the blather.

Eat meat pies, follow footy, change your name,
work on the haircut and the accent:
lie low and take your time.
Quietly celebrate that first arrival
in the memory of departure, as if
a visa were a birth certificate.
Neighbours in *terra nullius* call it home.

Remembering Enna

Now, as refugees from war in the Maghreb
are drowning in the Sicilian Channel,

and refugees from war in the Levant
are sinking off the Aeolian coast,

beating the border between Latin and Greek,
on the route that carried slaves and oryx

to the stadia, I remember Enna,
where Proserpine was first taken by Dis.

One Sunday, I strolled up Via Roma,
the spine of the hill holding the city

above deep green fields and shining rivers.
After a cool chiaroscuro circuit

of the Chiesa dell'Addolorata,
I stood in the shade of the loggia,

alongside an elegantly suited
Fiorentino. (He had the *gorgia*.)

The sun was high. On both sides of the *strada*
trattorie, *ristoranti*, *barbieri*

were open for business and busy.
Coffee and rosemary floated in the air.

Families were on the *passegiata*,
I could distinguish *dame di compagnia*

among the young women and their suitors.
Turning to the *Toscano*, eager to share

my African enjoyment of the scene…
"*Arabi!*" he growled. "*Tutti Arabi!*"

Welcome to Europe

1 BAHNHOF

Die Freifrau at the *Bahnhof* under rain
replays in memory a game of bridge:
der Baron facing her across the green
laid down his cards like paint to mark a street,
and could not understand his partner's rage,

but saw it in her knuckles glowing white
against the baize. The dull cold of concrete
foretells the vaulted chapel's draughty aisles,
and from the railway restaurant piling plates
mix with the feral scent of breakfast honey.

For young colonial guests her Christmas smiles
are well prepared. She will let them feel all
the sad kilometres of their journey
until their bags, laden on a trolley,
convert the greying station to a mall.

Outside, Romanian chauffeur holds his doze,
flexes his threadbare coat like movie mail,
wakes only at the bidding of the old
Baronin, whose bearing revokes the years,
the stark stigmata of the Reich, as though

sleek Astrakhan and sheer mantilla could
annul a dark fatal commitment. At least we know
that in the station yard there is a car
to take us to the *schloss*. A porter waves,
hesitantly clearing the breathy air.

2 SCHLOSS

Hereditary chamberlains lived and worked
in a fortified court, which they enlarged
with rampart and moat to this four-pointed
Renaissance castle. That's the eastern wall:
the portico's new. Welcome to our home.

From here the Hawk's Black Company of foot
marched to the Peasants' War and afterwards
we had to rebuild the *schloss*. The old church
in the fields is Lutheran now: angels
adorn our hardy chapel in the vaults.

A *Baronin* led this reformation.
These portraits, even the medieval,
date from a good year, 1700.
In the Enlightenment the four towers
received their onion domes. At this corner

the Margrave installed the first flush toilet.
Arches of sandstone replaced the wooden
drawbridge. Now the ivy covers the ditch.
Our airfield's hidden in mist: we're under
a flight path here. The runways looked like roads

and the hangars like farm buildings. Those Yanks
outstayed their welcome. Now our boys are back.
Things don't change much in a few centuries.
That clock tower's the *Kolonialschule*:
our Syrian refugees are processed there.

Salvation Creek

The tide is high. I have paddled
here out of the wind and weather

of the sound, seduced
by the modesty of the landscape,

the vestigial palms, memories
of rainforest veining the bush.

Through clear water, scattered rocks
cast their shadows on sand.

This is the only way to float,
rowing backwards up Salvation Creek.

Summer Now

Up early for a swim you call me from
our naked bed to see the python
coiled on the front steps
of our offshore home

into a firework. Or a hose? Out on
the bay, blown off course, visiting
like a bishop, the black swan
rests on the drift. Wakening

to the shallows, she raises her red beak.
Wings shake to show the chalky
trailing edge. From its stride the livid
body rises into the sea mist.

Rumours of bushfire. Stretch to sniff
the air, shade your eyes in a salute
to smoke. Read headlines
and horizons only.

In these deep suburbs, hot-to-the-touch
garden swings are too heavy
for the breeze. The dog sleeps
on the trampoline.

Sunbather

On the quiet cricket field, in the last
days of summer, mid-afternoon, no chill
on the air, she has spread her beach towel

over the unmown grass and stretches now
beneath a white straw hat, shades and an open
face-down Penguin waiting at her side.

Making my way along the tarmac path
that rings the field, I cross the polluted
water of the lagoon, its surface scratched

by moorhen, coot and grebe. Solemn purple
gallinule patrol the rabid bank. Downstream,
grey heron and white forage in the shallows.

On a high pole, osprey's abandoned nest
holds like pick-up sticks among dark floods.
Heading for home, I cross the bridge again

to the late daylight of the early field,
unpeopled now. In one low shaft of sun
a shadowed imprint lingers in the grass.

V

SONNETS

The Ceremony in the Garden

– for a wedding

One telling of the story of all things
springs in a garden of another's planting:
air blossoms there, the whole earth sings;
even at height of noon the light is slanting.

In time a cold north wind or scent of honey
leads from the garden to the world of stone.
Gathering what will serve us on our journey,
we face the fall together and alone.

Candles and music weigh among our baggage,
engines and ceremonies make us feel at home:
love is the load that lightens all our voyage

till night's new sky surrounds us like a dome.
Then from our tents of time we hear the sea
sing that we leave the garden to be free.

CLV

– for Howard Felperin

There is a character in all men's lives
that holds his hand beyond the point of death;
bears no evasion, no error forgives,
witholds his period until bate of breath.
This quality of men is in their deeds,
graving their acts and monuments in time;
and in their words, ready to whoso reads,
there is a property in every rhyme.
Nor can the printer hide the lines of life,
from face to foot the poet marks his page:
in actors' voices playing bliss or strife,
it is the playwrights' virtue lights the stage.
    Then hold my book, and hear me bear a part,
    conn'd in the tiring chamber of my heart.

Nativity

Lilies are breaking to the water's edge:
the caves and colours echo Cappadocia,
but for the stern surrender of the sea,
the sullen sun, the wind's chastening speech.

Tall awkward riders haunt the misty beach.
Are they merchants or acrobats? The star
has left this idle sky, we are too far –
too southerly to reckon on its reach.

Weighted with gifts, three academicians
dispute in patience at the stable door.
The carriers and shepherds sing like Phrygians.

Across the lilies and the cyclamens
they cast long shadows from the sand, those four
implacable pale horsemen on the shore.

News

Some of the townships had run short of rations,
rumours of typhoid ran through the locations;
despite official warnings to the nations,
there seemed no reason to control the passions;
occasionally trains arrived at stations;
some frequencies proclaimed the latest fashions,
others demanded generous donations,
offering relief to new and strange compassions.
Deep in the suburbs there was talk of fire,
housewives and widows whispered in the town.
One danger passed: the bare electric wire
no longer menaced. Slowly the dark came down.
It became necessary to face survival
before we started thinking of revival.

The Surfboat: Elegy

So, Palinurus of the last resort,
sweep with your spindrift voice the strokes and bowmen,
survivors of a sly and gallant court
bearding the windmill waves and clouds of omen.

Kevlar and fibreglass for pine and cedar;
aluminium for the balm of kauri;
reading horizons in the time of radar,
you will not see the shipwreck of the story

(the salt young body in the fresh lagoon,
casting his light and courage like a spendthrift).
Who cries for help beyond the foamy zone
when old eyes of the beach are on your craft?

The boatman's art outlives necessity:
until the next wave there is no more sea.

Trombone

  – for an African jazz pioneer

A one, a two, a three – and for the first phrase
flowering into a bar a line appears
to find a tune, falling or rising, lays
down a beat, to meet the slide that hears
an air beyond, sounding below the bell,
ringing around our ears, against the teeth:
so la ti, singing now, and we can tell
something to count on now, something beneath.
We breathe together, and our history
is still a favourite of Mozart,
starts in the time of Dorsey, leads a parade:
melody matters in the mind and heart,
runs with saliva to the water key:
we live as if we were what we have made.

Vivaldi's Starlings at Marianhill

This mercy seat is hard as a monk's bench
but we are here to hear spring's singing bird
called up by strings and flute and harpsichord.
In summer, calling cuckoo, dove and finch

find their gap before the storm. In autumn,
hunters' horns and hounds and guns surprise
the dawn. Even the chilly sharp reprise
allegro of the winter wind's return

through the secure door of the chapel
cannot blow away the cold's recurring
joys: in this last season, a devout couple
of shiny red-winged starlings, hovering

above, against the clerestory wall,
fly, improvising on their two-note call.

NOTES

p26 | Sunday Morning
• Blaauwkrantz Bridge: the Blaauwkrantz Bridge on the railway line between Grahamstown and Port Alfred was the scene of a great railway disaster on 22 April 1911
• *Abantu Bamlambo*: the spirit-people of the Kowie River

p28 | At Nongqawuse's Grave
• Although 'Nongqawuse' is the accepted transcription of the name of the Xhosa prophetess, it is spelled 'Nongqause' on the plaque at the gravesite

p59 | The Emigrants
• Macka's: McDonald's, the fast food chain

p60 | Remembering Enna
• Chiesa dell'Addolorata: Church of the suffering Madonna in Enna, Sicily
• *Fiorentino*: Florentine
• *Gorgia*: guttural pronunciation characteristic of Tuscany
• *Strada*: street
• *trattorie, ristoranti, barbieri*: trattorias, restaurants, barbers
• *passegiata*: promenading in your best clothes
• *dame di compagnia*: companion women, chaperones
• *Toscano*: a man from Tuscany
• *Tutti Arabi!*: all Arabs

Printed in the United States
By Bookmasters